Political Jokes of Leningrad

Collected by
ARIE ZAND

Photographs by Vladimir Sichov

Introduction by Alex Beam
Moscow Correspondent
McGraw Hill World News

SILVERGIRL, INC.

Political Jokes of Leningrad
ISBN 0-941432-01-7

First Printing August 1982

Silvergirl, Inc.
P.O. Box 4858
Austin, Texas 78626

All photographs by Vladimir Sichov/*Black Star*

Typesetting and Production - The Composing Stick, Austin, Texas

INTRODUCTION

With great secrecy, I had been smuggled in to a performance of the Soviet Union's "baddest" punk rock group, Aquarium. Banned in city after city, they shook the tiny world of Soviet rockdom by performing at the 1980 Tbilisi Rock Festival in t-shirts plastered with obscenities. Huddled among a conspiratorial group of die-hard Aquarium fans, I watched with fascination as their frazzle-haired lead guitarist, flush in red tights and a cutaway dinner jacket, bounced like a ping pong ball around a makeshift stage inside an obscure Moscow publishing house. "I'm dedicating our last song to the one real hero of Soviet youth . . ." the sweaty guitarist gasped into his microphone. ". . . Bob Marley!" Howls of approval from the audience. From there, he picked out the Jamaican reggae classic "Babylon" – with his *teeth!* "How do they get away with this?" I muttered to no one in particular. "Easy," explained my neighbor. "They're from Leningrad."

To better understand the jokes and photos in this book, it helps to have a feel for the city that spawned it. Leningrad—affectionately called "Peter" by its true admirers—is hip; Moscow is not. Leningrad was St. Petersburg, the vision of Peter the Great, a despotic genius whose greatest dream was to introduce Russia into the community of civilized nations. Moscow bears the stamp of such czars as Ivan the Terrible, typical of the despots that plunged Russia into the crippling mystical and intellectual isolation from which it is still trying to escape. Leningrad is the Venice of the North; Moscow is the Big Village. Leningrad is Russian; Moscow is Soviet. As the true Leningrader would explain it: if you're not in Leningrad, you're really not anywhere at all.

What's the allure? Leningrad is first of all elegant, neatly tailored around a symmetrical pattern of canals, with Peter's giant, verdant gardens dominating the city center. And if many Americans think of Russians as a frowzy lot who stir starchy soups with their fingers, nothing could further resemble today's Leningrader. Neither sex hoards kopecks on personal appearance. Leningrad's Nevsky Prospect is the USSR's only showcase for western fashions, such as disco bags, moon boots, and Adidas knock-offs. In comparison, Moscovites resemble ambulatory mushrooms, chuffing grimly from store to store on Gorky Street, packed into Moskvichka overcoats of the Dzerzhinsky era, capped with the traditional village kerchief.

Recently, Soviet television broadcast a newsreel on the Leningrad boot factory, Skorokhod (literally, Quick Walk), the largest in the country. Factory managers bragged of their efforts to keep pace with fashion in the West, of their modern manufacturing techniques, and of their impressive sales figures throughout the country. However, it emerged that sales in and around Leningrad were nil. "Why should I wear *local* boots?" sniffed one shapely Leningrader interviewed on camera. She lifted her fur coat to show the millions of television viewers a pair of handsomely styled beige moon boots, neither made nor legally sold in the Soviet Union. "When it comes to shoes, I prefer Finnish or Italian." Eat your hearts out, hicks.

It would follow neatly for the purposes of this brief introduction if Leningrad could lay claim to the country's best jokes, but in fact the jokes skillfully retold here belong to the rich trove that is shared by Russians all over the country. Jokes, or *anecdoty,* are the homemade glue that binds together all Soviet citizens in their dislike for the empty falsehoods of the government's long playing propaganda machine. In company, the first few jokes emerge after several rounds of drinking, like little secrets. By the time tea is served, the jokes start to flow, and flow, and flow. During one drunken evening, I remember our Armenian host had guided us through several broad categories of jokes: Stalin jokes, Brezhnev jokes, emigration jokes and jokes about Georgians (a local treat.) At three in the morning, he rose, swaying, to announce a new round of *anecdoty:* "And now . . . jokes about camels!"

It is surely no accident that this book comes at a historic moment in Soviet humor, the transition from jokes about Brezhnev, which dominated the 1970's and early 1980's, to jokes about "Andropka," or "Andropian," that last touch supplied by a small clique of jokesters who insist that Yuri Andropov's Armenian parents Russified their name at the time of the Revolution. This book contains all the classic jokes of the Brezhnev era, perhaps the Golden Age of *anecdoty.* Brezhnev's rough-hewn style, and the progressive deterioration of his mind and body kept the gagsters at work around the clock. What now? Whither Soviet jokes?

Not surprisingly, the first few months of the Andropov period have witnessed a resurgence of jokes in which Brezhnev is dead, for example the Brezhnev in Hell joke:

> The Devil has welcomed Brezhnev to Hell, and has invited him to choose his own punishment. To this end, the Devil provides a guided tour of available tortures: Hitler is being flogged by vengeful Jews, Karl Marx is forced to live under socialism, etc. Finally, in a tiny grotto removed from the main chamber of horrors, Brezhnev spots Vladimir Lenin making passionate love to Marilyn Monroe.
>
> "There, that's what I want!" Brezhnev gestures excitedly towards the pair. "Lenin's punishment."
>
> "You idiot!" the Devil snaps back. "That's Hell for Marilyn Monroe!"

But that joke belongs to the past. So far, jokesters and caricaturists are having similar problems with Andropov. He is admittedly nondescript, without noticeable deviations from the norm of appearance. Unlike Brezhnev, Andropov speaks a crisp, economical Russian that is not easily lampooned. Inevitably, the humorists have focused on Andropov's immediate past as chief of the KGB security police, with predictable results. One line now making the rounds in Moscow: "I try not to think too much about Andropov, and I hope he does the same for me." Another current joke has an aide announcing the arrival of a Vietnamese student delegation in the General Secretary's anteroom. Andropov looks up from his desk, and, peering over his spectacles, mumbles mechanically: "Take them away."

Alex Beam
Moscow, winter, 1983

Party Solidarity

Menshikov, a long-time member of the Party, is asked: "Comrade, why didn't you attend the last party committee meeting?"

"Well," said Menshikov, "if I had known that it was the last one I would have brought my whole family."

What is meant by the 'international solidarity of the proletariat?'

It is when there is no meat in Leningrad and butchers in Warsaw have gone out on strike.

In Leningrad there is a rumor that the schools will soon teach three foreign languages. English and Hebrew for those who plan to leave, and Chinese for those who plan to stay.

283
СРЕДНЯЯ ШКОЛА
ЛЕНИНГРАД

An old man stands against the empty window of a fish store and recollects aloud: "I remember in this corner of the window there was always trout, here they used to put caviar, there . . . smoked fish, perch, carp, but then . . . "

A militiaman, overhearing this reminiscence steps forward and says gruffly, "But then, what, comrade?"

The old man is surprised. Cautiously, he says, "Well, then, at that time, I was not able to understand why one needed all those smelly fish anyway."

Comrad Krylov has left Leningrad on his first trip to the West. From each country he sends a postcard to his family.

1. Best regards from free Poland. Krylov.
2. Best regards from free Hungary. Krylov.
3. Best regards from free Bulgaria. Krylov.

And the last one: Best regards from France. Free Krylov.

What is required of a Jew who wants to join the Party?
Recommendations from three Arabs.

Two old acquaintances meet on a Leningrad street.

"Where is Yuri now?" asked one. "He used to tell such marvelous jokes about the Party committee meetings. Didn't he live across from the prison?"

"Oh, he's still in Leningrad," said the other man. "He just moved across the street."

Two crocodiles are dozing on a river bank. Suddenly, one of them jumps up and cries: "Freedom to Angela Davis!"

"Take it easy," the other one cautions.

The first crocodile lies down and immediately falls asleep once again. But a moment later he quickly jumps up yet another time and shrieks: "Freedom for Chilean patriots!"

The second one is thoroughly irritated and confused now.

"Would you shut up!" he says.

They sleep again, at least until the first crocodile pushes himself up onto his feet and screams: "Down with American imperialists!"

"Oh my God!" exclaims the second crocodile, finally realizing what has happened to his companion. "He must have had a communist for lunch!"

The motto of Soviet coal-miners: Each real communist must be underground.

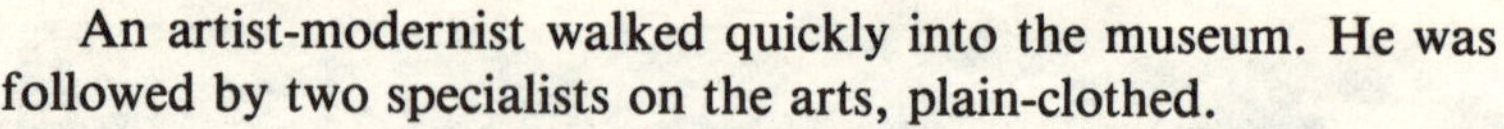

An artist-modernist walked quickly into the museum. He was followed by two specialists on the arts, plain-clothed.

This is a question often debated by Leningrad's Marxist intellectuals. Is it possible to build a genuine communist society in just one isolated capitalist country like Iceland, for example?

The consensus is that, certainly, it is possible. But what on earth has Iceland done to us?

The Bulgarian Prime Minister received journalists in his office. They were surprised at the variety of telephones on his desk. "With this phone I speak to France," said the Prime Minister pointing to the green one, "by this one—to Greece, by this—to Turkey, by this—to Italy, by this . . ."

"But which do you use to talk to Moscow?" asked a journalist.

"Oh, for that I use these headphones," said the Prime Minister.

An international group of biologists has just completed a cooperative study of elephants in Africa. Upon their return to their respective countries each member of the group reported their findings.

The German scientist wrote ten volumes entitled: 'A Short Introduction to the Science of Elephants Observed in their Natural Habitat.'

The French representative's work: 'The Sexual Life of Elephants.'

The Russian: 'The Marxist Interpretation of Elephant Science.'

The Bulgarian: 'The Bulgarian Elephant as the Loyal Companion of the Noble Russian Elephant.'

An American and a Russian argue about which country has more freedom.

The American says: "I can walk in front of the White House and shout 'Down with Carter,' and not one thing will happen to me."

The Russian, on the other hand, boasts: "I also can walk in front of the Kremlin and cry 'Down with Carter,' and nothing will happen to me either."

Marxist Dialectics

Petka was an adjutant of the reknowned Civil War hero, Chapaev. Once he asked the great man: "Comrade Chapaev, could you please explain to me the meaning of 'Marxist dialectics'?"

"Well Petka," replied Chapaev thoughtfully, "it's really a matter of science. However, I'll try to explain it as simply as I can by using examples. Imagine, there are two people standing in front of a bath house. One is dirty and the other clean. Who, do you think, will enter the bath house?"

"The dirty one, of course," said Petka.

"No, you are wrong. You see, the dirty man is like a pig. He is accustomed to living in filth like an animal. He never washes. But a clean man is a different sort. He knows what it is to be washed. So he will enter the bath house. Understand?"

"Yes, certainly," said Petka.

"Now, another example. Imagine, there are two persons standing before a bath house. One is dirty and the other is clean. Who will enter the bath house?"

"The clean man, of course."

"No, no. Wrong again. Clean is clean, and the bath house is for the dirty. So the dirty man will wash himself in order to become clean. That's what the bath house is for, after all. Got it?"

"Yes," said Petka. "I think I understand now."

"Now here's a third example. Imagine that there are two persons standing in front of a bath house. One is dirty, the other is clean. Who will go inside?"

"Who the hell knows?!"

"Petka, now you've got it. This is exactly the meaning of Marxist dialectics."

A student is taking an oral exam in Soviet History. He is apparently doing well until the professor asks him: "When was the Bolshevik Revolution?"

"I don't know."

"Well then, who wrote DAS KAPITAL?"

"No idea."

"Who was Comrade Lenin?"

"I never heard that name before," said the student unabashedly.

"Well, young man, you must be able to tell me this: Who is Comrade Brezhnev?"

"Br- Br- who??"

"Listen, where are you from?"

"I'm from the village of Petrovka in Siberia . . . "

The professor is thoughtful now. "Petrovka, Petrovka . . . Sounds like a heavenly place."

An American, a Frenchman, and a Russian met. They discussed obedience to authority in their respective countries. After the American and the Frenchman had presented their views, the Russian invited them to a typical Soviet factory. This is how he was going to make his point:

He gathered all the workers together and announced, "Comrades, starting today you will no longer be paid for your work."

The workers immediately shouted, "Hurray!"

The following week, before his American and French friends, he again assembled the workers. Now he announced that ". . . beginning tomorrow we will work compulsory twelve hour shifts." The workers enthusiastically cried, "Hurray!"

And a week after that he brought the workers together for a third announcement. "In addition to the previously announced changes, there will be yet another. From this day forward, at the conclusion of each shift ten of you, chosen arbitrarily, will be hanged." And once again everyone cried, "Hurray!" However, this time one old machinist did raise his hand timidly.

"What's the problem?" asked the Russian manager.

"I just wanted to know if we must bring our own rope or will this be supplied by the factory?"

The results have been announced of a competition for the best design for a monument to the great Russian poet of the nineteenth century, Pushkin. A special commission awarded the Third Prize to a design entitled: ‘Pushkin With A Volume Of Karl Marx.’ The Second Prize was given to the entry entitled: ‘Pushkin With A Volume of Lenin.’ And finally, the First Prize was awarded to the design: ‘Lenin With A Volume of Pushkin.’

There is a great military parade in Moscow. Among the dignitaries on the reviewing platform are Alexander the Great, Julius Caesar, and Napoleon. The infantry is marching in perfect array behind sophisticated motorized armament. Alexander the Great is obviously impressed. "With an army such as this I could have conquered the world," he says enviously.

Caesar, who appears overawed, is speechless. And Napoleon, who is busily reading a copy of Pravda, does not reply.

Formations of jets fly overhead and swoop down over the reviewing stand. Caesar exclaims: "If I had machines like those I'd bring the entire world to its knees."

Napoleon is still very absorbed in Pravda and does not respond.

Finally Alexander asks him: "Why don't you watch the parade? This is truly a magnificent army."

"Perhaps it is," says Napoleon. "But this newspaper is really amazing as well. If I had had it, the world would never have known about Waterloo."

The head of a Soviet trade delegation to Hungary notices, to his surprise, a sign above the entrance to a large building in Budapest: "Ministry of the Navy."

"How come," he asks his guide, "you have a Naval ministry in a country that does not even have access to the sea?"

"That shouldn't seem particularly remarkable to you," replied the Hungarian guide. "Doesn't the Soviet Union have a Ministry of Culture?"

It is a well-known fact that before communism reaches its final and most perfect form it must first pass through a preparatory period of socialism. Just now, however, the Soviet Union is in an intermediary stage not described by Marx. This stage is called 'alcoholism.'

During an international track and field competition, a Soviet hammer-thrower, Kuriatin, established a new world record. A journalist asked: "Comrade Kuriatin, how did you manage to throw your hammer that far?"

Kuriatin replied: "Give me a sickle, and I'll throw that even farther."

A caller to Radio Armenia asked this question: "How is it now with meat in Armenia?"

The commentator's reply: "With meat everything is alright, *without* meat everything is awfully bad."

A Citizen writes a question to Armenian Radio:

"What came first, an egg or a hen?"

Armenian Radio answers gloomily, "Before there was everything."

Anastas Mikoyan is the Talleyrand of Soviet communism. He is the only Politburo member to have survived all sorts of purges, changes in power, and reversals in policy. In fact, he was in the Politburo for approximately fifty years, longer than anyone else. This story is told about him:

One overcast day he walked from his Kremlin office.

"It's raining," the doorman said to Mikoyan.

"Perhaps."

"It surely is, Comrade. You'd better get an umbrella."

"Don't worry, my friend. Somehow I'll manage to walk between the drops."

A fairy says to a Czech: "I can fulfill three wishes, whatever they are. But remember, only three!"

"Alright," says the Czech enthusiastically. "My first wish is that China invade Czechoslovakia."

"OK," says the fairy. "If that's what you want, consider it done. Second?"

"My second wish is that China invade Czechoslovakia."

The fairy is surprised. He thinks how easy this will be. "I'll do that, of course. And your third?"

"My third wish is that China invade Czechoslovakia."

"Fine, if that's what you've got your heart set on. I'll fulfill all three of your wishes. But, tell me, why do you want such an affliction upon your own country? The Chinese will invade it three times!"

"Of course, that's true. But I think it's worth it. By doing this the Chinese will have to cross Russia six times!"

Tolstikov, leader of the Leningrad Party Committee and well-known for his anti-semitism, was appointed Soviet Ambassador to China. When his plane landed in Peking he walked from the cabin onto the tarmack where a group of Chinese dignitaries awaited him. He looked at them and said: "Ah, you kikes, . . . always something. Now you're squinting."

How does a clever Russian Jew talk to a stupid Russian Jew?
From New York, by telephone.

Soviet Economics

A tenet of Soviet economics: The relationship between the rouble, the dollar, and the pound sterling is constant. A pound of roubles is always equal to a dollar.

In Leningrad an official Soviet brothel for foreigners has been opened. It was equipped with the most sophisticated sauna and hot tubs, modern furniture, and audio system. However, even after months, it has failed to become profitable. The Directress of the brothel is summoned before the city Party Committee.

"Comrade Morokova, the Fatherland desperately needs foreign currency. Your brothel is our last chance to balance our foreign accounts. We have met all your requests, and, yet, you are still unable to make a profit."

"Forgive me comrades, but I myself cannot find an explanation for our failure. The building is superb in every way, the rooms are perfectly private and elegant, and the girls are real beauties. All are Russians and all are ideologically correct . . . Party members since 1917. But those damn Africans just aren't interested in them."

What would happen if the Communists took the Sahara Desert?
In a few years even sand would be in short supply.

Leningrad Graffiti

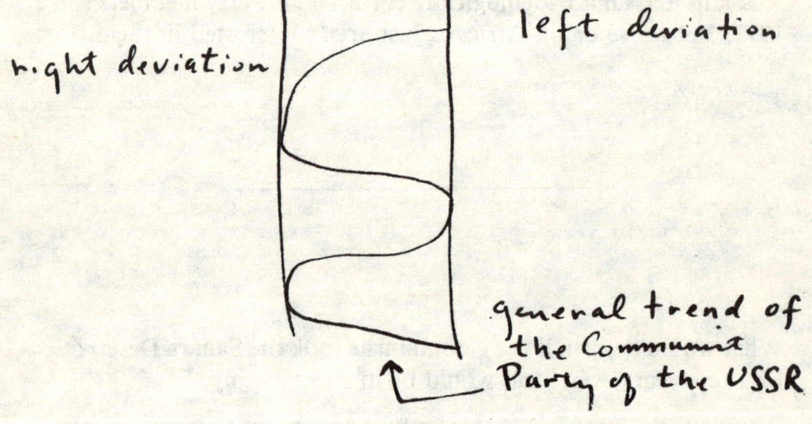

A delegation from the Committee of Soviet Women visited several North African nations. On her return, one of the members of the delegation told her friend about the trip.

"First we arrived in Morocco. Rabat was beautiful. We had an especially wonderful breakfast there . . . tender crabs' legs in oranges and almonds."

"And then?" asked her friend.

"And then we were brutally raped."

"All of you?" asked her companion, aghast.

"All, except Maria. Next we stopped in Algiers. That was truly magnificent. A dinner of lamb with mint and sesame seeds . . . and the wine! It was first-class."

"And then what?"

"And then we were fiercely raped."

"All of you?"

"All, except for Maria."

The friend is incredulous.

"We finished the tour in Alexandria. In the hotel there we bathed in ancient springs with almond soap and finally covered ourselves with lime oil."

"It sounds scrumptuous. But what happened then?"

"We were mercilessly violated."

"All of you?"

"All, except Maria."

"And why not Maria?"

"I guess she is very shy."

Comrade Brezhnev

"Comrade! Have you heard the story about Brezhnev's body floating down the Moscow River with a knife plunged through his heart?"

"No, I haven't."

"Neither have I . . . but isn't that a good beginning?"

The Order of Lenin is the most coveted award bestowed on the heroes of the Soviet Union. Nevertheless, Leonid Brezhnev receives it almost yearly, like a ritual. As a consequence of this, the government has passed the following resolution:

"In recognition of the numerous and glorious Orders of Lenin awarded to Comrade Brezhnev, we, The Presidium of the Supreme Soviet of the Union of Soviet Socialist Republics, bestow the Order of Lenin on the Order of Lenin."

Late one evening the doorbell rang in Comrade Brezhnev's apartment. He got out of bed, pulled on his pants, donned his jacket, and went to the door. As he opened it he took a card from his pocket and read: "Who is it?"

Comrade Brezhnev was on a holiday in the south. He was lying in the sun on a beach reserved for party officials. Other members of the Politburo were lying around him. His eyes were closed and he appeared to be just dozing off when a small dog ran up through the sand and licked his heels. A smile of contentment appeared on Brezhnev's face. After a few moments the dog, wagging his tail joyfully, walked behind the First Secretary and began licking his ass. Without opening his eyes, Brezhnev gratefully acknowledged, "Well comrades, this is really too much."

It is known that in 1968 there was an assassination attempt on the life of Party First Secretary, Leonid Ilych Brezhnev. It is also known that a certain Lt. Popov fired a shot intended for the First Secretary but succeeded only in wounding Brezhnev's chauffeur. Political historians are still disputing the facts surrounding this incident. One group maintains that Lt. Popov's arm was thrown off by certain persons in the crowd grabbing for his pistol and shouting: "Give it to me! Let me do it!" Another group familiar with the near-tragic event asserts that the chauffeur was only wounded after the bullet ricocheted off Brezhnev's head.

At the inaugural ceremony of the Moscow Olympic Games Comrade Brezhnev, leading an array of dignitaries, mounted the podium. When everyone was finally settled in his proper place, the First Secretary solemnly unfolded his speech and began to read the first line.

"O-O-O-O," his voice rang out confidently.

An aide anxiously touched his arm and whispered, "Leonid Ilych, you're reading the Olympic emblem on the letterhead. Go on to the next line!"

Comrade Brezhnev ordered a group of high level space scientists and spacecraft designers to come to his office.

"Comrades," he said, "we are falling behind the Americans in exploration of outer space. This situation is intolerable. So we have decided that unless there is an immediate and marked improvement in the quality of your work we will gather you up, altogether, and send you to the sun."

"Comrade First Secretary," a spokesman explained, "that's impossible. The temperature there is extremely high. We will burn to ashes."

"Of course, you won't burn," he retorted contemptuously. "Do you think we in the Politburo are just fools? We will launch you at night."

A special commemorative stamp with a picture of Brezhnev has been issued. It is a fine likeness, yet there have been many complaints that the stamp does not stick on envelopes. An extraordinary commission was formed to investigate these complaints. Their findings corroborated the widespread suspicion that the stamp would not stick because people were spitting on the wrong side.

Relaxing after a rough day at the Politburo, Comrade Kosygin asked Comrade Brezhnev, "Lyonya, would you like to hear an American riddle? I'll bet you all the roubles in Rostov you'll never solve it. Listen! He's my father's son but he's not me. Who is it?"

Brezhnev furrowed his brow in deep concentration and finally replied, "I give up. What's the answer?"

Kosygin, beaming with satisfaction, "It's my brother!"

"That's a good one," snorted Brezhnev. "But don't run off. I've got to tell this one to Comrade Podgorny." He turns to Podgorny. "Hey, Kolya! Listen to this American riddle. He's the son of my father, but he's not me. Who is it?"

Podgorny, who was anxious to make an impression, thought carefully for a while until he finally had to concede: "I just don't know."

Brezhnev was exceedingly pleased with himself: "It's easy Kolya. It's Kosygin's brother."

During one of their telephone conversations, Brezhnev confided to President Carter: "Can you imagine that last night I had the strangest dream: A great red banner was flying on top of the White House, and the letters on the banner said, in Russian: LONG LIVE COMMUNISM." Brezhnev laughed and wondered aloud, "What could that have meant?"

"I don't know," said Carter, "but I have dreams like that too, sometimes. Why just last night I dreamt that there was a tremendous red banner over the Kremlin, but I couldn't read what the letters said."

"Why not?" asked Brezhnev.

"Well, I can't read Chinese," Carter replied.

In the morning, the sun shines into Comrade Brezhnev's study in the Kremlin and whispers to him tenderly:

"Good morning my dear Comrade Brezhnev! How are you feeling today?"

"Thank you, sun. I'm fine, just fine."

In the afternoon the sun, floating in the sky, sees Brezhnev walking in a garden and says:

"Good afternoon, most illustrious comrade. I'm so glad to see you again."

"Thank you, my friend," Brezhnev replies. "Your kindness to me is very touching."

But later in the evening the sun did not greet Brezhnev when he walked along the Moscow River after dinner.

"What is wrong, sun?" Brezhnev asked. "Why have you not greeted me this evening?"

"Go to hell, Leonid Ilych! I'm already in the West."

A foreign journalist is granted an extraordinary interview with First Secretary Brezhnev. The journalist is determined to discover more about Brezhnev, the man, not just the politician. He asks, "Do you have any hobbies?"

"Yes, of course," replies Brezhnev. "I collect jokes."

"How many jokes do you have so far?" asks the journalist.

Brezhnev thinks this over for a moment and then responds, "Oh, about two labor camps full."

One more proof that the earth is round: All of the shit we have been throwing to the West for so many years is now returning to us from the East.

The Director of a ball-bearing plant received a call from the Leningrad Party Committee. In one month he could expect a delegation of American labor union representatives to tour his plant. The Director immediately asked the lathe-operator, Ivanov, to come to his office.

"Comrade Ivanov," he said, "in one month an American labor delegation will visit our plant. They are certain to ask all sorts of questions, and, no doubt, they will ask about our Jewish problem. Of course, we fired all of those kikes long ago. There's not a single one left. So I am asking that you, Comrade Ivanov, will assume the identity of a Jewish worker. From now on your name will be Rabinowitz. Everything will be arranged; we will even give you new documents."

Ivanov hesitated. He appeared stunned.

"I understand how disgusting it will all be for you, but remember, it will only be for one month. And then you can be our Comrade Ivanov once again. Please, will you do this for us? Your sacrifice will not go unrewarded."

Ivanov reluctantly agreed. He received new documents. Everyone was instructed to refer to him as Rabinowitz.

When the American delegation arrived they were shown around the plant. Afterwards they were fed herring, cabbage, bread, and tea. Then the Director entertained their questions in his office. He was prepared for the worst. Sure enough, one of the Americans asked, "What about the Jewish problem in your plant?"

"The Jewish problem?" said the Director feigning surprise. "There is no such problem. Many Jews work here. They are respected members of our proletarian community. We have no so-called 'Jewish problem.' Perhaps you'd like to meet one of our typical Jewish workers? That is easy enough. For example, there is Comrade Rabinowitz, a lathe-operator, a party member, and one of our best workers. I will invite him here."

The Director turned to the Chief Engineer at his side and said, "Please ask Comrade Rabinowitz to come up to the office."

The Chief Engineer looked uneasy. "I'm sorry, Comrade Director, but Rabinowtiz has already emigrated to Israel."

How does an Armenian interpret so-called 'Soviet Internationalism"?

He will tell you that it is when an Armenian, a Russian, a Jew, a Tatar, and a Georgian embrace one another as genuine brothers and then go off together to beat the hell out of an Azerbajdzanian.

A Jew who happens to be a tailor is brought to KGB headquarters. It is 2 A.M. as he is driven through the empty streets in a 'Black Maria.' When he arrives he is asked:

"Comrade Rabinowitz, do you have any relatives abroad?"

"No. Not a single one."

"But we have found here," said the interrogator, presumably holding up Rabinowitz's 'dossier,' "that you have a brother in the U.S. He is an engineer at an aerospace facility."

"Well comrade, that is not exactly correct. You see, I know who you mean, but he is not actually my brother. Not a full brother. And besides, I was only two years old when he left Russia."

"Do you want to establish correspondence with him?"

"Oh no, not me. He is perfectly unknown to me. I am not responsible for anything he's done so perhaps I'll just go home now."

"Please, sit down. We here at the KGB would like you to write him a letter nonetheless."

"Alright, fine," says Rabinowitz. "I'll go directly to my apartment and compose a long letter."

"But Comrade Rabinowitz, why wait until you get home. You can write it here, right now."

"Oh sure, of course," says Rabinowitz who is anxious to be cooperative. "I'll write it here."

Rabinowitz sits at a table. He is given paper and a pen. He begins to write:

Dear Abram,

Finally I have found the proper time and place to . . .

A lieutenant has just completed a session of political indoctrination with a group of new recruits for an elite Army-corps. He reports to his colonel who asks, "Well, how did it go Menshikov? Were there any provocative questions from the men?"

The lieutenant appeared somewhat confused. "Well, there was possibly one provocative question," he said.

"Well, tell me! What was it?" snapped the colonel.

"It was just that onc fcllow askcd mc why sputniks fly in spacc without ever falling to the earth."

"And how did you answer him, Menshikov?"

"Comrade Colonel, I gave him an elusive answer."

"Well, what did you say?" asked the colonel, obviously irritated.

"I just told him—'Go to hell, man!' "

A Leningrad district party committee assigned an official to find a replacement for a rabbi who had gotten twenty-five years at Kolyma. More than a month passed without the selection of a new rabbi. The party committee summoned the official for an explanation.

"Well, Comrade Petrov, what's the problem? Why haven't you found a new rabbi?"

"Well," said Petrov uneasily, "I have been unable to find a suitable candidate. So far, the only ones I've interviewed are either Jews or they aren't party members."

A Georgian is informed that coffee prices have soared 200%.

"I don't care. I drink coffee now and will continue to drink coffee."

Gold has increased 150%.

"That's not a big deal. If my wife wants gold earrings, she'll get them."

Furniture has become 100% more expensive than before.

"Believe me, I still won't be eating on the floor."

In Moscow, it's now 25°C, in Tbilist . . .only 15°C.

"Oh, my God! Intolerable! Those bastards in the Kremlin do just whatever they want."

Soviet Agriculture

The chairman of a kolkhoz near Gorky addresses the milkmaid, Marya.

"Listen Marya, I've got a message for you from the area party committee. It states that tomorrow a journalist from 'Pravda' will come to research a story about the successes of our collective farm. They direct you to give him an interview.

"Comrade Popov, what do you mean, 'an interview'?"

"Well, to be perfectly honest, I'm not really sure myself. But, in any case dear, be sure to wash up."

In the early thirties, in a kolkhoz, the members worked hard and long. Because of this and much luck they were able to accumulate a profit of one million roubles. At a general meeting of all members, they discussed what ought to be done with the money. Someone suggested that they build a new pig-pen, another that they construct a new school. Suddenly, an old peasant took the floor.

"Comrades," he said, "let's use this money to buy plywood."

Everyone was astonished. A young worker spoke up. "Old man, you're crazy! What will we do with a million roubles worth of plywood?"

"Don't you understand?" said the old peasant. "We've got a million already, we buy the plywood, build an airship, and then fly the fuck out of here!"

Is it possible for an elephant to get a hernia?

Yes, if it will try to lift Soviet agriculture.

Why is there a shortage of meat in the Soviet Union?

Because the courageous Soviet people have moved toward Communism in great strides. And the cattle could not keep pace.

Four reasons why Russian agriculture falls behind: 1) winter, 2) spring, 3) summer, and 4) autumn.

Comrade Brezhnev will be awarded the Nobel Prize for agriculture. He has planted wheat in Kazakhstan and gathered the harvest in Iowa.

What is the difference between Soviet and Western paralysis?
Soviet paralysis is more progressive!

Russian Xenophobia

How will the Chinese launch their first Sputnik?

300 million of them will hold a sling-shot, and 400 million will pull a rubber band.

First secretary Brezhnev has apparently consulted a reknowned 'sleep specialist' after suffering from this recurring nightmare: He sees a Pole sitting in Red Square eating matzo balls with chopsticks.

What will be on the Soviet-Chinese border in 1990?

Wc don't know, but hopefully the Chinese-Finnish border will be quiet.

Overheard in a Leningrad streetcar: "Have you heard that the Chinese have already come very close to Moscow?"

"No. I hadn't heard a thing!"

"No wonder. They're going barefoot."

Middle-Eastern Affairs

During the 1967 Sinai War, a Soviet military 'observer' saw ten fully-armed Egyptian soliders fleeing from an Israeli with only a pistol. In vain he tried to stop them. When he finally did catch up with them he was furious. "Hold it, you idiots! Why are you running?!! There is only one Jew behind you."

"Yes sir, apparently that is true," one of them replied. "But we don't know exactly which one of us he is chasing."

The Arabs explain that they did not actually lose the 1967 Sinai War. They merely used a strategy suggested to them by the Russians: lure the enemy deep inside your territory and then wait for the frost.

During the 1973 Arab-Israeli War a company of Egyptian paratroopers is dropped in the Sinai, presumably in the vicinity of a single Israeli soldier. Two days later, three wounded Egyptians . . . what is left of the crack paratroop company . . . straggle into the Egyptian headquarters. The commander is infuriated. He will be demoted. Perhaps shot. "How could this have happened?" he cries. "There was only one Jew out there!"

"No Commander," one of the paratroopers hesitatingly replies, "intelligence totally mis-informed us. There were two of them."

In Leningrad there is a surplus of Cuban sugar. It has been utilized in many innovative ways. In fact, when it is added to Russian yeast by certain entrepreneurial moonshiners, it forms a 'Friendship Liqueur.'

In Vietnam, the Americans, for the first time, shot down Russia's most technologically advanced aircraft. Although the plane completely incinerated, the pilot was able to parachute to safety. He was discovered by an American patrol and then taken to Saigon for questioning by high-ranking Intelligence officials.

"What type of plane do you fly? What is it called?"

The pilot, who is a genuine Soviet patriot, remained absolutely silent. Although he was severely beaten, he still did not answer.

"What is the range of your plane, its maximum altitude, speed?"

They beat him brutally, but still no answer.

"What type of fuel do you use, your ETA, your ETD. With what sort of weaponry is the plane equipped?"

They tried electric shock, every sort of hideous torture the capitalist devils can invent, yet the pilot, a hero of heroes, still did not utter a single word.

The following day the Vietcong launched a sudden attack against the American Intelligence compound. The pilot was rescued by the guerillas and eventually returned to Moscow. Finally, in a military hospital there he recuperated from his awful ordeal. Friends from his squadron visited him.

"Hey Vasya, what was it like to be a prisoner with the Americans? Rough?"

Vasya pulls himself up in bed and responds gravely: "Listen comrades . . . you've got to study the equipment, know it inside and out. They ask a lot of questions."

Stalin Rehabilitated?

Comrade Lenin is dressing for an important meeting of the Central Committee. He is unable to find his pants so he asks his wife: "Nadja, where are the gray pants I brought from Switzerland?"

"Volodya darling, I have no idea."

So he opens one closet after another.

"In this closet—no, in this—no, in this—no, in this—oh, hello Comrade Stalin—no, in this closet—no."

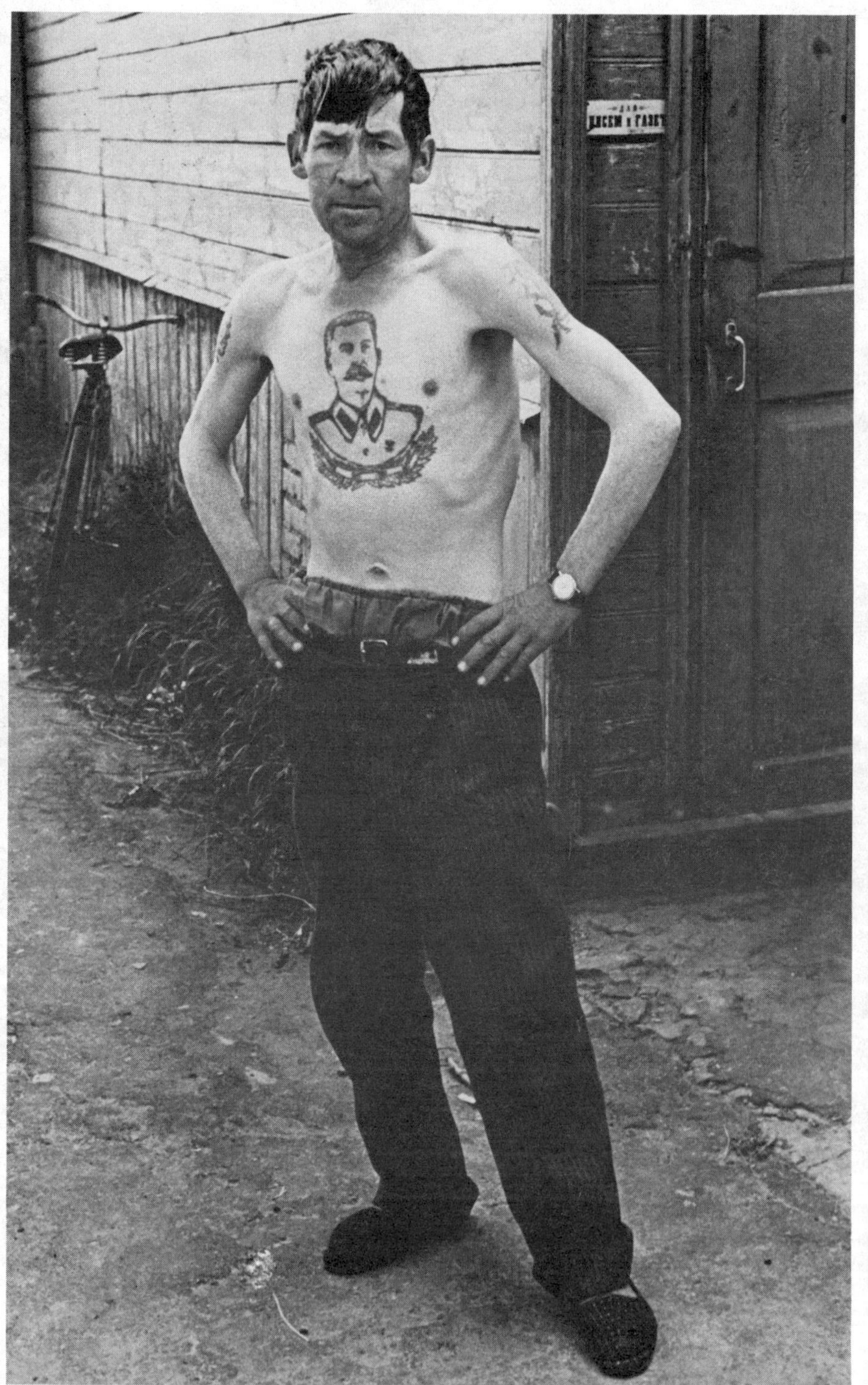
ДЛЯ
ПИСЕМ И ГАЗЕТ

Intellectuals Speak Out

What is the difference between socialism and capitalism?

Capitalism is based on exploitation of a human being by another human being, but socialism is just the opposite.

Although it is said that capitalism is rotting, it certainly smells good!

Who invented socialism, workers or scientists?

Workers, of course! Scientists, we are sure, would first have tested it on hamsters.

Communist Party theoreticians in Leningrad have considered the following question: What is the difference between the Congress of the Communist Party of the Soviet Union and the Plenum of the Communist Party of the Soviet Union?

Their conclusion is that whereas the Plenum is of historical significance, the Congress is of universal historical signifcance.

In Leningrad certain intellectuals debate: 'What is a neutron bomb?' Their conclusion: It is a great vodka booth with no line behind it.

A young Russian writer, a member of the Academy (yet almost a dissident), is walking down the street. He meets a friend who asks: "Hey, how are you? How are things?"

"Bad, gloomy," he replies.

"What's the matter? Is there some news?"

"Well," the writer says, "I got a new apartment in the center of Moscow. Seven rooms."

"That's great!"

"Oh no, everything is bad, really rotten."

"Well, is there other news?" asks the concerned friend.

"I did get a summer house. It's in a good spot, and I paid only 60,000 for it. But that doesn't really matter."

"Excellent!"

"No. No, everything is gloomy."

"How can you say that? Something must have happened."

"I guess you don't know. I bought a new car. Mercedes . . . it runs well."

"Fantastic! I'm glad for you." A long pause. "But there's still something eating at you. Tell me, what is it."

The writer shakes his head. Tears, like little lakes, grow big in his eyes. "I guess it's just that our people live so damn bad."

A Soviet factory worker chooses to sit in front of the TV and relax. He turns to Channel 1. Famous actors are reading passages from Brezhnev's latest book. The worker quickly switches to Channel 2 just in time to see a commentator read the text of a Brezhnev speech: "I am honored to be allowed to speak before this, the congress of Kolkhozniks after . . . ." Changing over to Channel 3, the worker hears another commentator describe: "In his speech yesterday before the Mongolian delegates, Leonid Ilych Brezhnev declared that . . . ." Disgustedly switching to Channel 4, the worker learns that ". . . today in the Kremlin, our dear and revered Comrade Brezhnev . . . ." Finally, he turns desperately to the final channel. From the screen a KGB major glares threatening toward him and shouts: "You bastard, you'd better stop switching these channels!"

At a Soviet underground missile base deep in Siberia officers are sitting in the Control Room playing cards. Suddenly an enraged colonel bursts in. He shouts: "Who pushed the Green Button?"

Everyone is silent, stunned, frightened.

"I ask you again, who pushed the goddamn Green Button?!"

No answer.

"Listen I don't give a damn about Australia, but I want to know which one of you pushed that button."

One Soviet citizen advises another on what action he must take in the event of an American nuclear attack: “Comrade, cover yourself thoroughly with a white sheet and crawl slowly to the cemetery.”

“But why slowly?” he is asked.

“In order not to spread panic.”

At an international medical conference, a group of physicians shared their experiences informally between the delivery of the scholarly papers.

A French physician lamented: "Our problem is that we successfully treat a patient's rheumatism, yet he dies from cancer."

A Canadian physician agreed: "The same thing happens in our practice. We treat a man of jaundice, but he dies of a heart attack."

A Russian physician angrily interjects: "Everything that you say is nothing but bourgeois ambivalence. We, in the Soviet Union, treat our patients, say, from pneumonia, and I can assure you that they die from pneumonia."

Towards Utopia

The highly respected Bureau of Statistics of the USSR has just released the results of a study of the average length of life in the Soviet Union. Just ten years, it is claimed. Seven years before school and three years after retirement.

They say, communism is our horizon. That's true. The closer you approach it, the farther it moves from you.

An American, on tour in Leningrad, slipped on a loose flagstone and fell into a pile of garbage. Angry, dirty and embarassed he complained to the tour guide.

"In my country such places are surrounded with red flags so that people are careful to avoid them."

"Well, we do the same thing here," answered the guide. "Didn't you notice the big red banners as you crossed the border into the Soviet Union?"

On a bright spring afternoon in a Leningrad park there is an intense discussion concerning the origin of Adam and Eve.

A Tatar asserts that Adam must have been a Moslem since it is believed by some Moslems that an apple is a magical fruit.

A French Communist visiting Leningrad claimed that Eve was French because it was his feeling that only a French girl would sleep with a man for an apple.

Finally the Lengingrader said that he believed, without any doubt, that they both had to be Russian. It was his contention that only Russians could be naked and barefoot and still claim that they live in Paradise.

What is the difference between the Soviet Constitution and the American Constitution?

The Soviet Constitution guarantees freedom of speech and freedom of gathering. The American Constitution guarantees freedom after speech and freedom after gathering.

It is said in Leningrad that after socialism a genuine Communist society will be built in Russia. And then internal passports will no longer include the hated infamous 'fifth paragraph' concerning nationality. However, it is suspected by certain cynics that this will be replaced by a paragraph that will ask: 'Your nationality *during* socialism?'

An old Jew sits on a crowded Leningrad streetcar. Suddenly a huge Russian with a face like a pink beach ball steps on his foot. The pain is severe, yet the old Jew says nothing. After a few moments though, it becomes excruciating. He can stand it no longer. Just as he feels he will faint, he asks meekly: "Comrade, please step off my foot. It is very painful."

The giant Russian explodes: "Ah, so it hurts you, you son-of-a-bitch!! Everything hurts you. A Russian man just can't find a place to put his feet. You bastards are everywhere, you grab everything, and you still demand even more. Now you'll see what I'm going to do to you . . . ."

An elegantly dressed, very distinguished-looking Russian with an intelligent face and kind eyes, has been sitting beside the old Jew. He has been reading Kafka and has been terribly troubled by what has been going on. At last, he is unable to stand it any longer. He addresses the angry Russian who stands above him.

"Well, sir, perhaps you had better step off his foot. After all, the kike has every right to his seat."

A sergeant in the Soviet Army is highly respected, not only as a soldier but also as a philosopher. In fact, he is able to combine the concepts of 'space' and 'time' in ways never before imagined by Western thinkers. An example:

He orders his men to dig a ditch from the fence until lunch time.

A Soviet citizen appears in the Immigration Bureau in order to obtain permission to go to his desperately ill uncle in America.

"My uncle is near death," he says. "Besides that he recently became blind and deaf."

"Listen," says the immigration official, "why don't you ask your uncle to come here to Russia instead of you going to America?"

"I'm sorry, my uncle may have lost his sight and hearing but he hasn't lost his brains."

An old man recollects how he once met Lenin:

"I was a small boy when my father worked in the Kremlin as a garbage collector. Once I was playing ball there and accidentally rushed into Comrade Lenin's room. He was just shaving, I think. I asked him, 'What are you doing, Comrade?' And you know that instead of slashing me with his razor, he simply replied, 'I am shaving.' Can you imagine? I will never forget that kind man."

Soviet Emigration

Rabinowitz, a Party member, chief engineer of a large factory, and decorated veteran of World War II, applied for an exit visa to Israel. He was questioned by the local Party committee.

"Comrade Rabinowitz, what's the matter? Why do you want to leave the Motherland? What is the reason for this?"

"Well, comrades, there is a reason, an important reason, but I've just happened to forget it now."

"Perhaps there is a problem at your work . . .?"

"Oh no! Everything's fine there. That's not the reason."

"Could it be then, dissatisfaction with your apartment?"

"No, not actually. My apartment is quite nice: ninth floor, five rooms, a view of the tractor factory . . . ."

"Would you like a greater salary? Is that it?"

"No. Actually, I am well paid. No problems there. I'm sorry but I just can't remember the real reason I want to leave."

"It's probably that you don't have a car. That's it, right?"

"But I do have a car. As a matter of fact, I just got a new Fiat . . . it's a beauty. The reason totally escapes me. This is very embarrassing."

"Then what is it that you want, you kike-face!!?"

"Oh, thank you," said Rabinowitz, "I think I just remembered the reason."

A well-known economic planner, party member, and decorated veteran of World War II, Abraham Moskovitz, applied for an exit visa to Israel. As a result of this he is asked to report to the local party committee.

"How could you, a prominent citizen, a party member, a War hero choose to go to that stinking Israel?"

"Well, it's not all it appears to be. I, personally, am strongly against it. But my wife wants to go, and you know how a woman can turn your life into hell."

"Moskovitz, listen to yourself! What are you saying. You supervise the work of three hundred and you can't deal with your own wife?"

"Actually, my wife isn't the worst of it . . . my in-laws . . . they are just driving me crazy. Every day it's the same thing: "Let's go, go-go-go-go . . . Israel, Israel, Israel . . . ."

"But during the War you were a regimental commander. You distinguished yourself in battle. And now you're giving in to your in-laws. This is impossible to believe."

Moskovitz shakes his head pathetically. "I guess I could handle it with my in-laws . . . and with my wife too . . . , but my children both of them . . . they're driving me crazy. Every day they cause a new scandal in the apartment. They just won't stay here, and that's all there is to it."

"Please, listen, Comrade Moskovitz, you have been a party member for forty years, and now you can't even explain things to your own children?"

Finally, Moskovitz throws his hands up in the air. "Comrade, what do you want from me? What can I do if I am the only Jew in the whole goddam family?!!"

СССР

Old Bolsheviks Reminisce

Since 1965 Party publicists have been trying to find someone who had participated in the famed Communist Free Labor Day of 1918 in which Lenin also took part. Finally, after tedious canvassing and re-canvassing of all Leningrad's districts, a stooped and wrinkled old man claimed that he had been there. He was asked to describe that day.

"Well," he recollected, "they drove us to a square somewhere near the Winter Palace. The wind and cold were awful. Most of the fellows shuffled off in their thin coats. Not me though. I sat back in the truck and smoked awhile. Suddenly, a short, bald fellow . . . who I later learned was none other than Lenin, our beloved leader . . . approached the back of the truck and called to me inside: 'Well comrade, will you help me carry away a great pile of wood?'

"He seemed like a fine enough fellow but, sure enough, I answered him: 'If you're looking for idiots, you'd better fuck off!' "

" 'Does that mean," he asked me very correctly, 'that you are not willing to carry wood?' "

" 'Well, no!' I said."

" 'Well, then, you will chop and saw trees!' he shouted."

"And what happened to you then?" the interviewer asked anxiously.

"Well, he was right. Just three days ago I returned from the camp."

On January 9, 1905 in St. Petersburg, Cossacks and soldiers attacked a group of workers demonstrating peacefully. This incident is known as 'Bloody Sunday.' Sixty years later Party historians actually discovered an old man who claimed he was a Bolshevik and had participated in the historic event. Although his memory was very clouded, he was able to recall the following about that fateful day:

"So we entered the square . . . thousands of us . . . unarmed workers . . . on our way to the Czar's Palace. As the group slowly made it's way across the square, we Bolsheviks kept reassuring them that . . . that . . . that . . . ."

"Well, what were you telling them?" asked the anxious historians. The old Bolshevik thought hard for a moment. "Ah. Yes, yes! I remember. Just then our commander ordered: "Cossacks, draw swords . . . ."

As everyone knows, the great hero of the Civil War, Comrade Chapaev, died while swimming across a river after his division had been routed by the Whites. A group of Pioneers managed to discover a 100-year veteran who claimed he was the last Bolshevik to see the famous hero alive.

"I was at the river's edge and could see him swimming. He was supposed to be a strong swimmer, but the great man was wounded. He could barely stay afloat. My heart cried for him."

"And what happened next Comrade?"

"Well, it's been 60 years . . . ."

"But what can you remember?"

"Not too much, except that just at that moment my colonel called to me: 'Ivanov, do you see that Red bastard in the middle of the river?' And as I sat behind my machine gun and inexplicably pulled the trigger . . . that was the last time I saw the heroic Comrade Chapaev."

In Lenin's Mausoleum, a father whispers to his son: "And before, Comrade Stalin was also lying here."

"Where is he now?" the boy asks.

"Well, he was taken away."

"And who took him away?"

"Probably his relatives . . .," the father said diplomatically.

"Do you mean this bald guy here is an orphan?"

An American, a Frenchman, and a Russian have come together in order to exchange stories about their countries.

The American says: "When my Mary sits on a pony, her legs rest on the ground. It's not because ponies are so small in America, but because my Mary has such very long legs."

The Frenchman says: "When I buy my Marie a new blouse and she puts it on, the buttons just pop off. It's not because we in France produce poor textiles, but because my Marie has such great bosoms."

Finally, the Russian says: "When I come to my job in the morning, I slap my Masha on the bottom. When I finish my work her butt is still trembling like jelly. But it's not that my Masha has such a fat bottom, but because we in the Soviet Union have a very short work day."

A village priest approaches the secretary of the local party committee with a special request. "Comrade Ivanov," he says respectfully, "our church needs renovation. Could you please issue us thirty buckets of paint?"

"Impossible! Not for a church," says Ivanov. "I have many other priorities."

"But Comrade Ivanov! The church of God looks like a shack and it reflects very poorly on your administration. Please allow us at least twenty buckets of paint?"

"Leave me alone! It's harvest time. Every moment is precious, and now you with your goddamn church."

The priest is resolute. "Please, have human feelings. Give me at least ten buckets."

"Get out of here," shouts Ivanov. "I won't give you anything."

"Alright then," says the priest. "Then I won't give you churchpeople for harvesting potatoes."

"So be it," retorts Ivanov. "But you won't get children from the Young Pioneers League for singing in the choir!"

"Well, if that's the way you want it . . .no more nuns to attend party members in the saunas."

"What?!! No more of those whores for the saunas! That's it, priest. Turn in your party card this minute!"

A Soviet pessimist and a Soviet optimist.

The pessimist says: "Russia has become such hell. Everything is so bad it couldn't become worse."

The optimist says: "It will, it surely will."

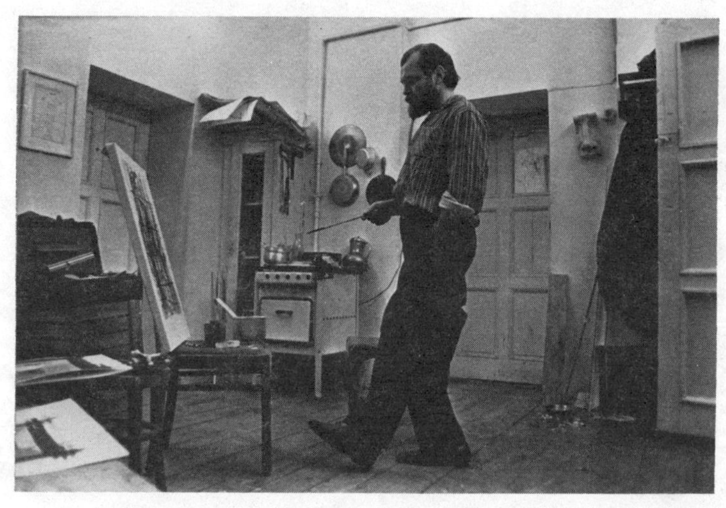

On the 100th anniversary of Lenin's birth, labor paid it's tribute. Industries throughout Russia released new products in order to commemorate this event. The Minsk Perfume Factory introduced a cologne named Eau de Lenin. The Soup Factory of Irkutsk kicked off its ad campaign for a new bean consomme called: Volley of the Revolution. And in Smolensk the Candy Works sold a life-size likeness of Lenin in Chocolate.

Three young Leningraders decided to join the Party. Each went off to the headquarters of his own district of the city. In the evening they met, as planned, on the steps immediately in front of the Winter Palace.

The first told his story proudly: 'I told the commission that before the Revolution my father had a store. Not as big as the Main State Department Store in Moscow, but nonetheless a store. And you know, they just didn't seem to care. So I was accepted into the Party.'

The second man said: 'I told them that before the Revolution my father had a factory. Not as big as Kirov's plant here in Leningrad, of course, but it was a factory nevertheless. And they accepted me as well . . . no questions asked.'

The third man was very puzzled. 'Then I don't understand what's wrong with me,' he said. 'I told them that before the Revolution my father had a brothel. Not such a big brothel as we have now, but a brothel. And they refused me!'

An American tourist boasts to a Russian: "I have three cars at home: I use one to go to work, another for my summer vacation, and the third is for travelling abroad."

The Russian replies self-confidently: "Well, I really don't need a car at all. I go to work on the subway. I go to my summer house by train. And as for foreign trips, well, I go by tank."

A priest sits on one of the bridges over the Neva River in Leningrad. He is reading a textbook of Hebrew grammar. A crowd of curious passers-by gathers around him. Finally a militiaman comes up.

"Listen priest what kind of disturbance are you causing here?"

"I'm only learning Hebrew," he confesses innocently.

"Why on earth do you need to know this?" the militiaman asks.

"Well, you see, I'm a sick man. It's true that I'll probably die soon. And when I do, I'd like to be able to speak to the Lord in his native language."

The militiaman can't help but laugh. He asks, "How can you be so sure you'll go to Paradise anyway?"

The priest nods knowingly. "Well, maybe I will and maybe I won't. But if I don't, I'm ready for that too. After all, I already speak Russian."

Father Dudko, arrested April, 1980.